JUNETEENTH

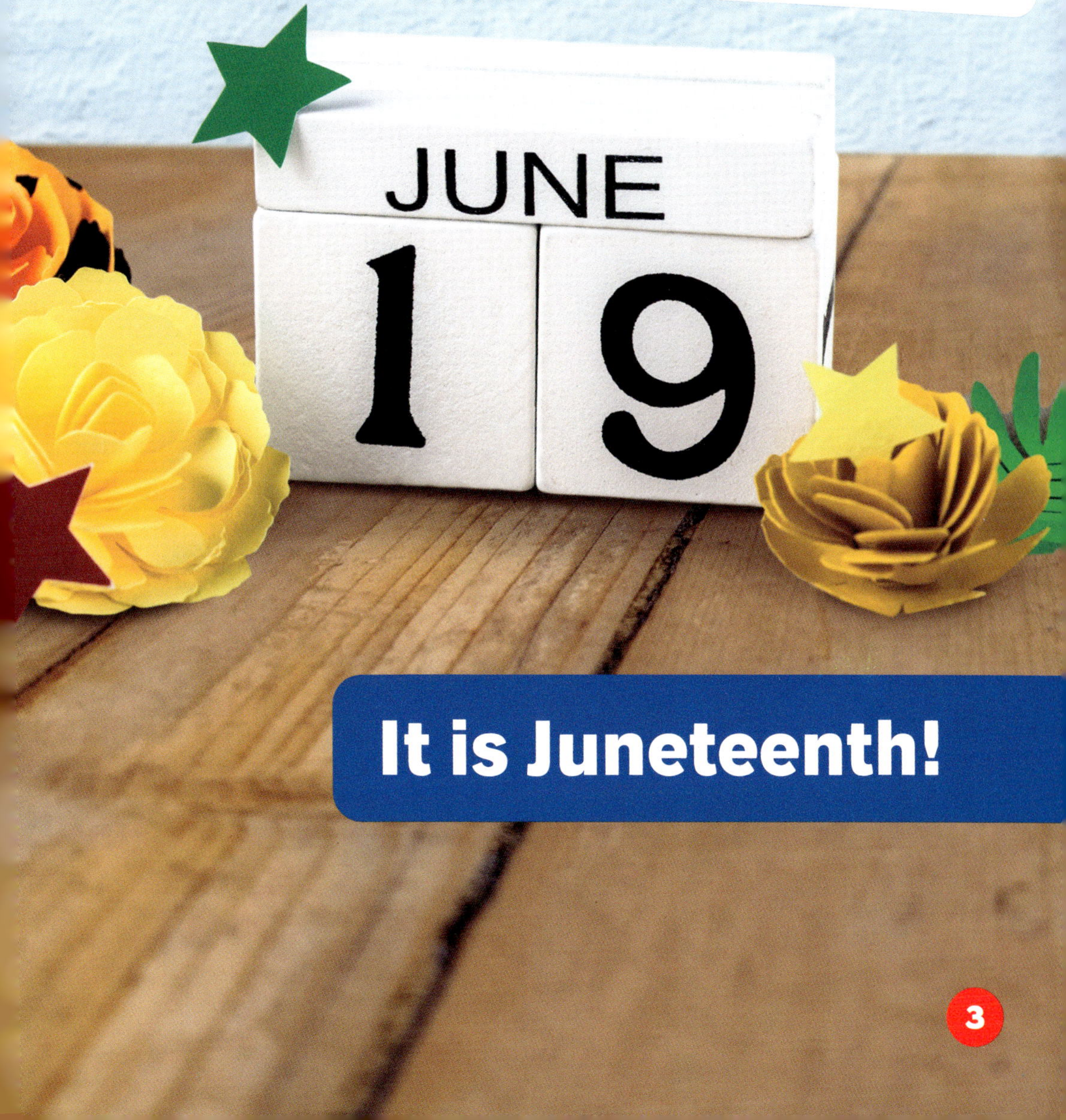

It is Juneteenth!

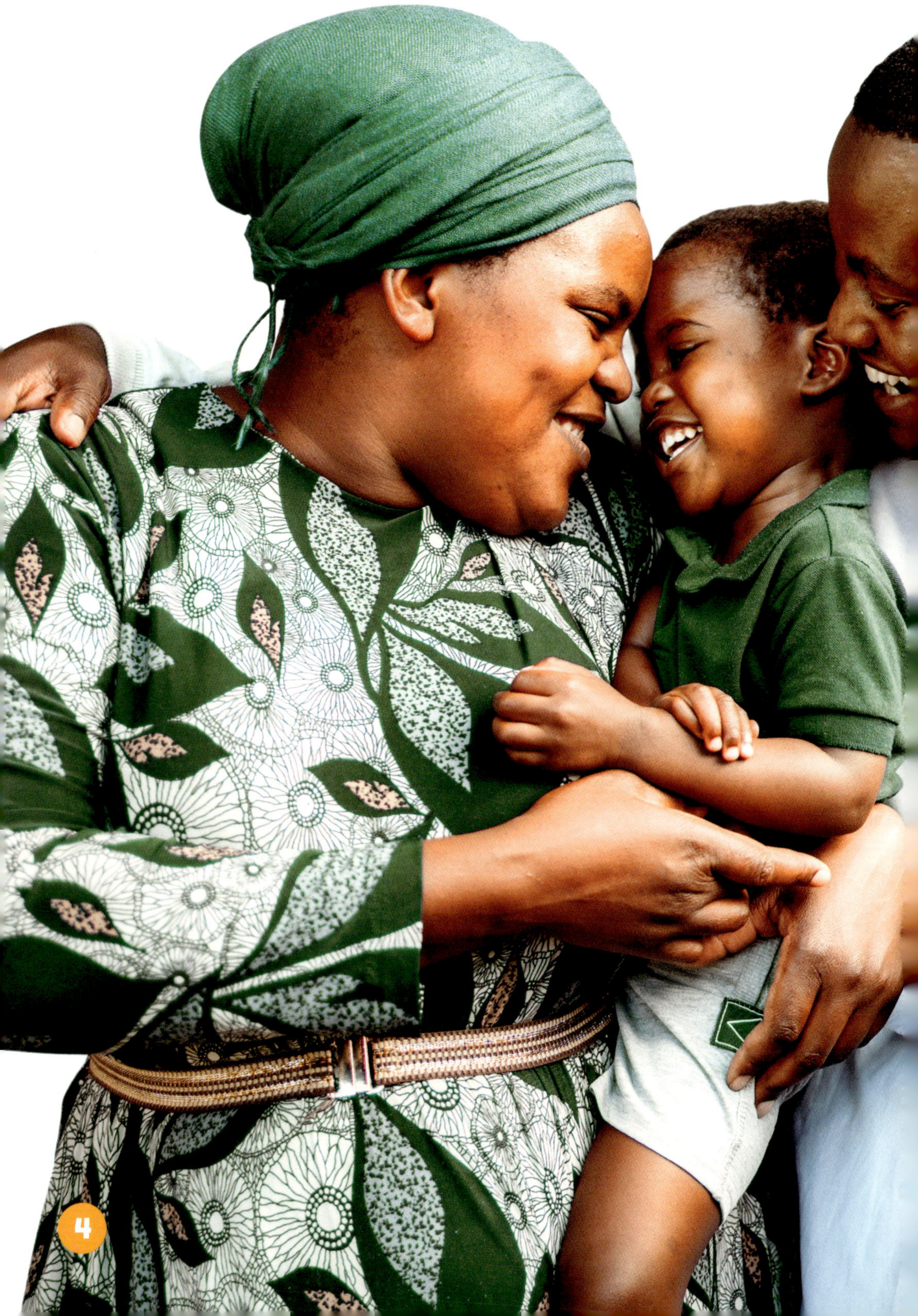

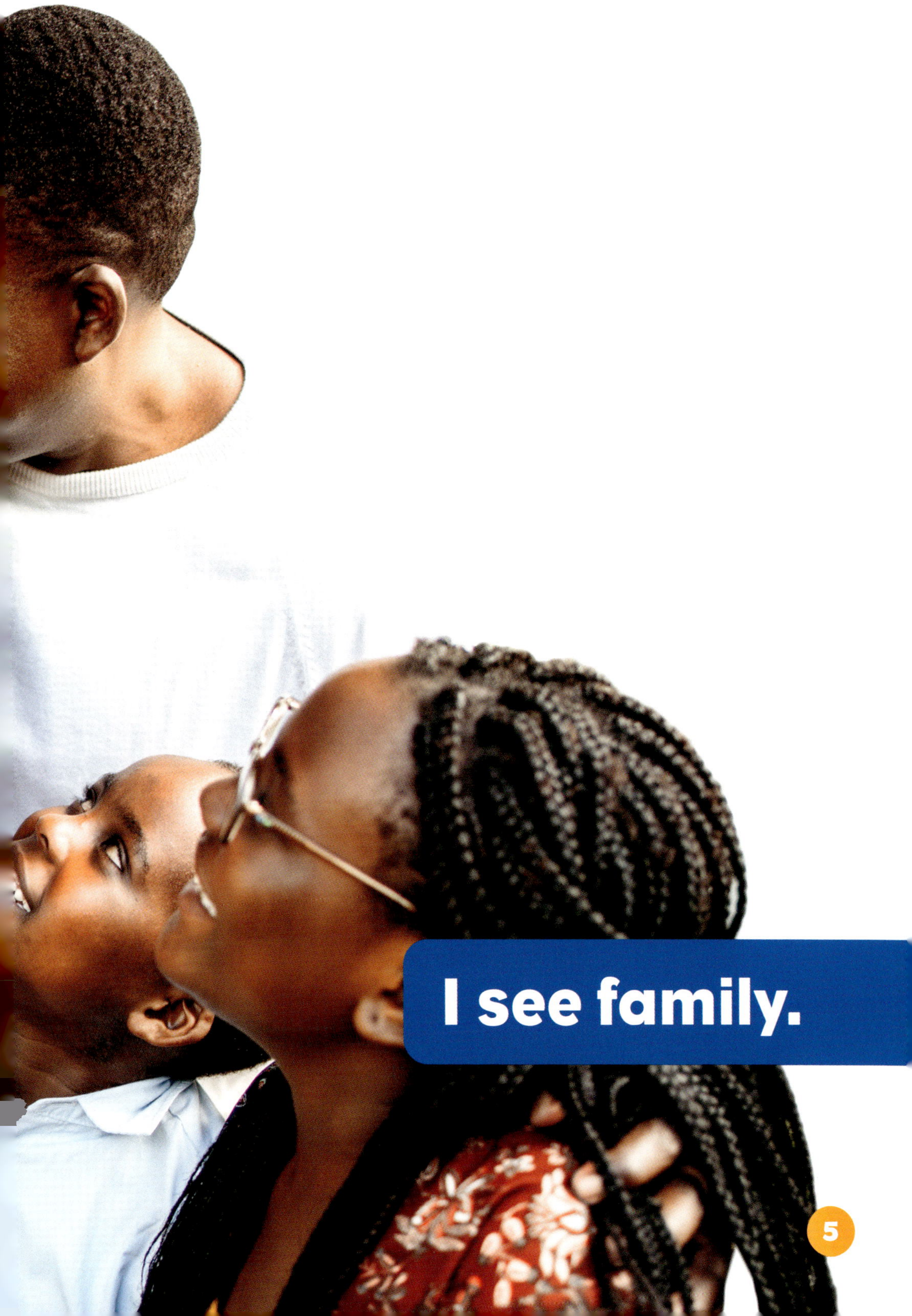

I see family.

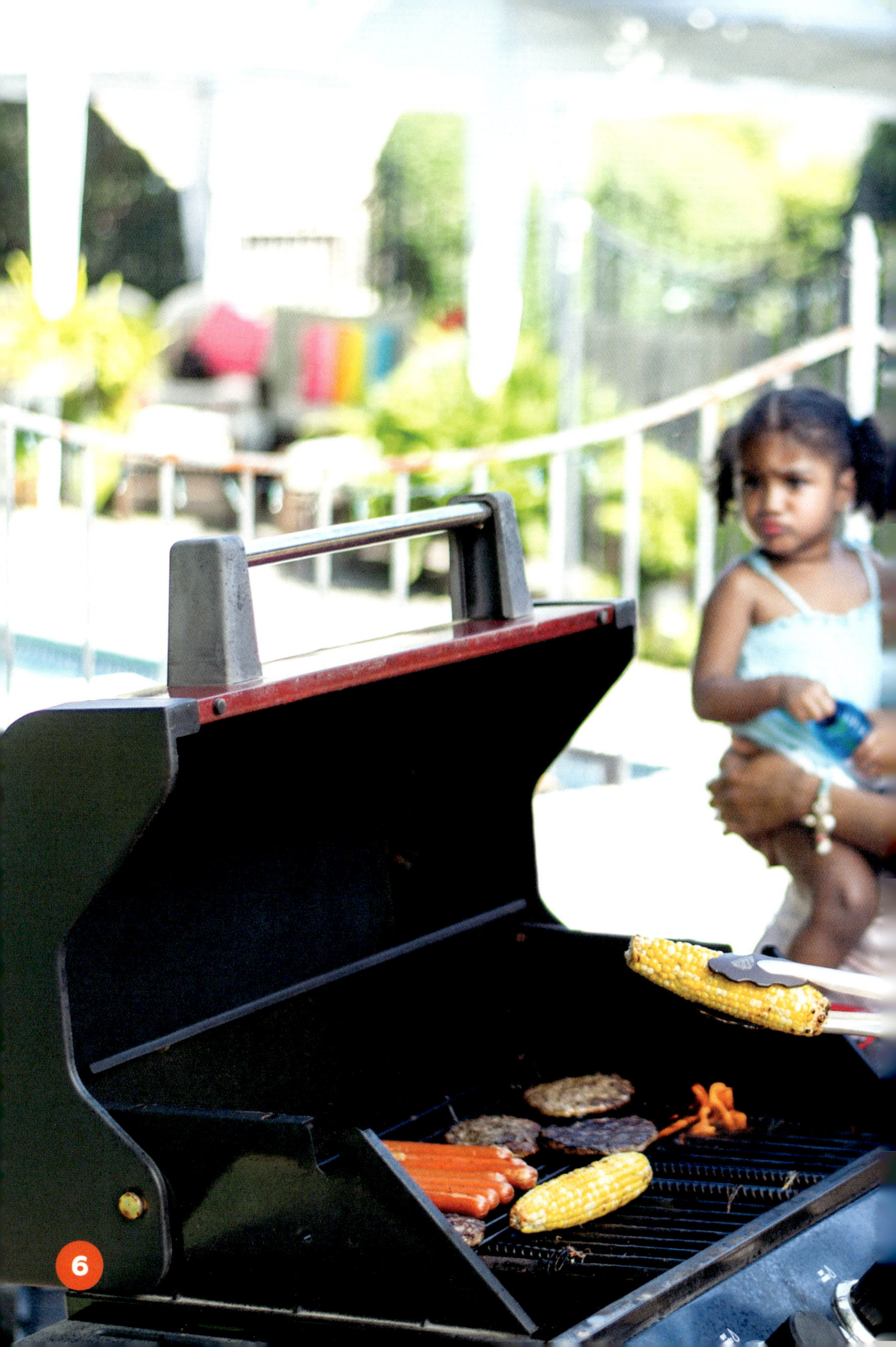

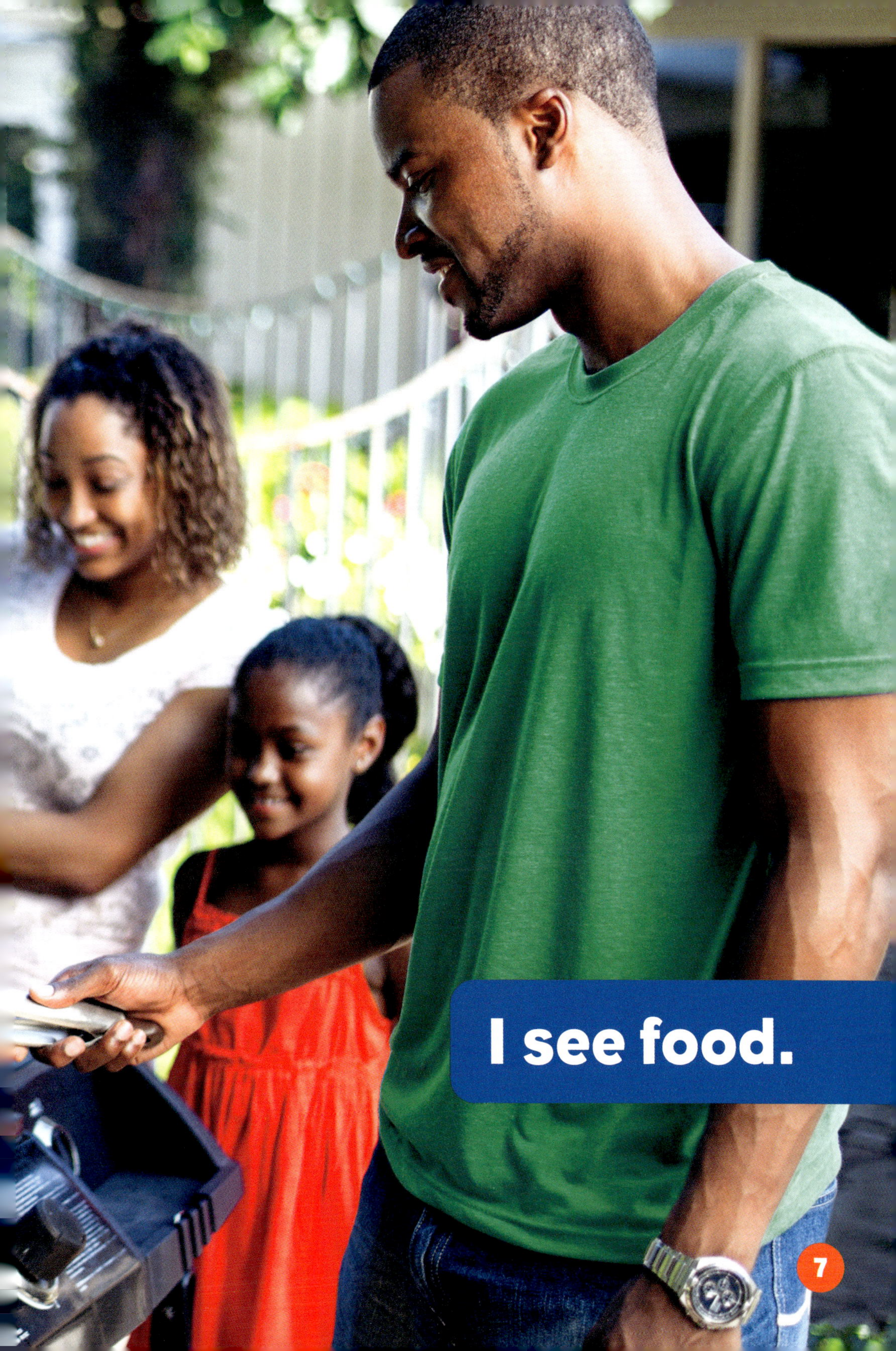

I see food.

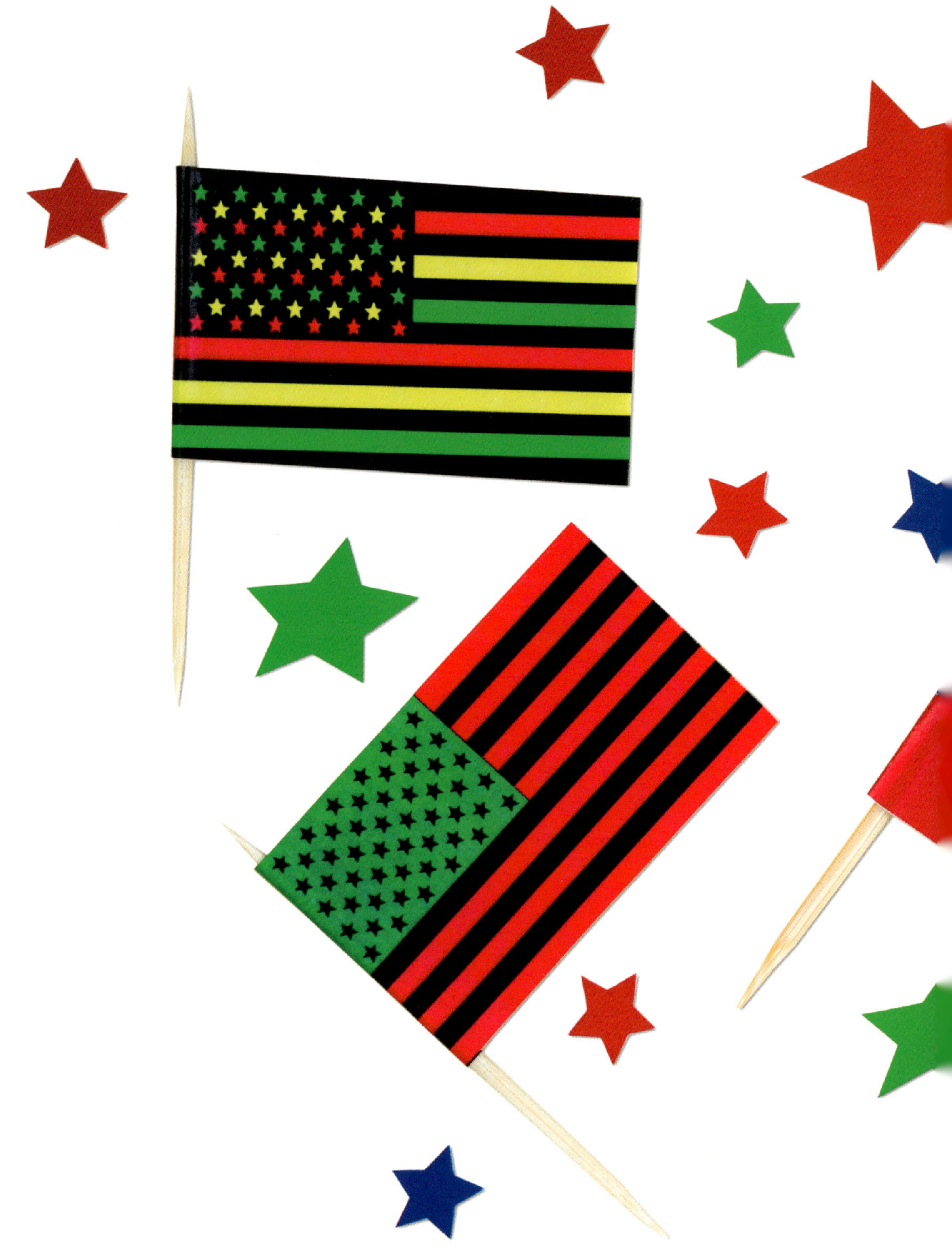

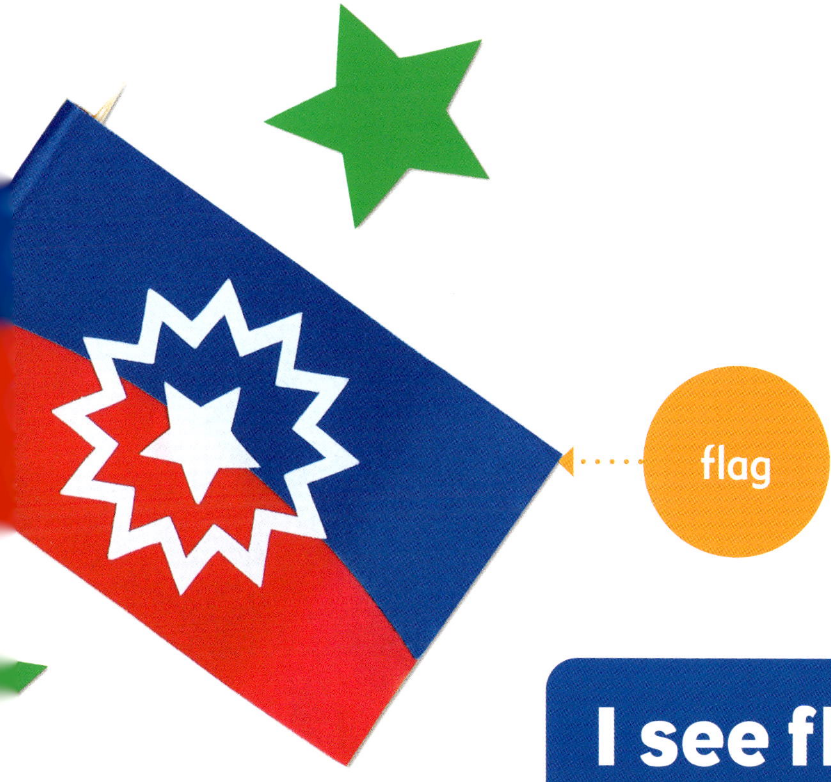

I see flags.

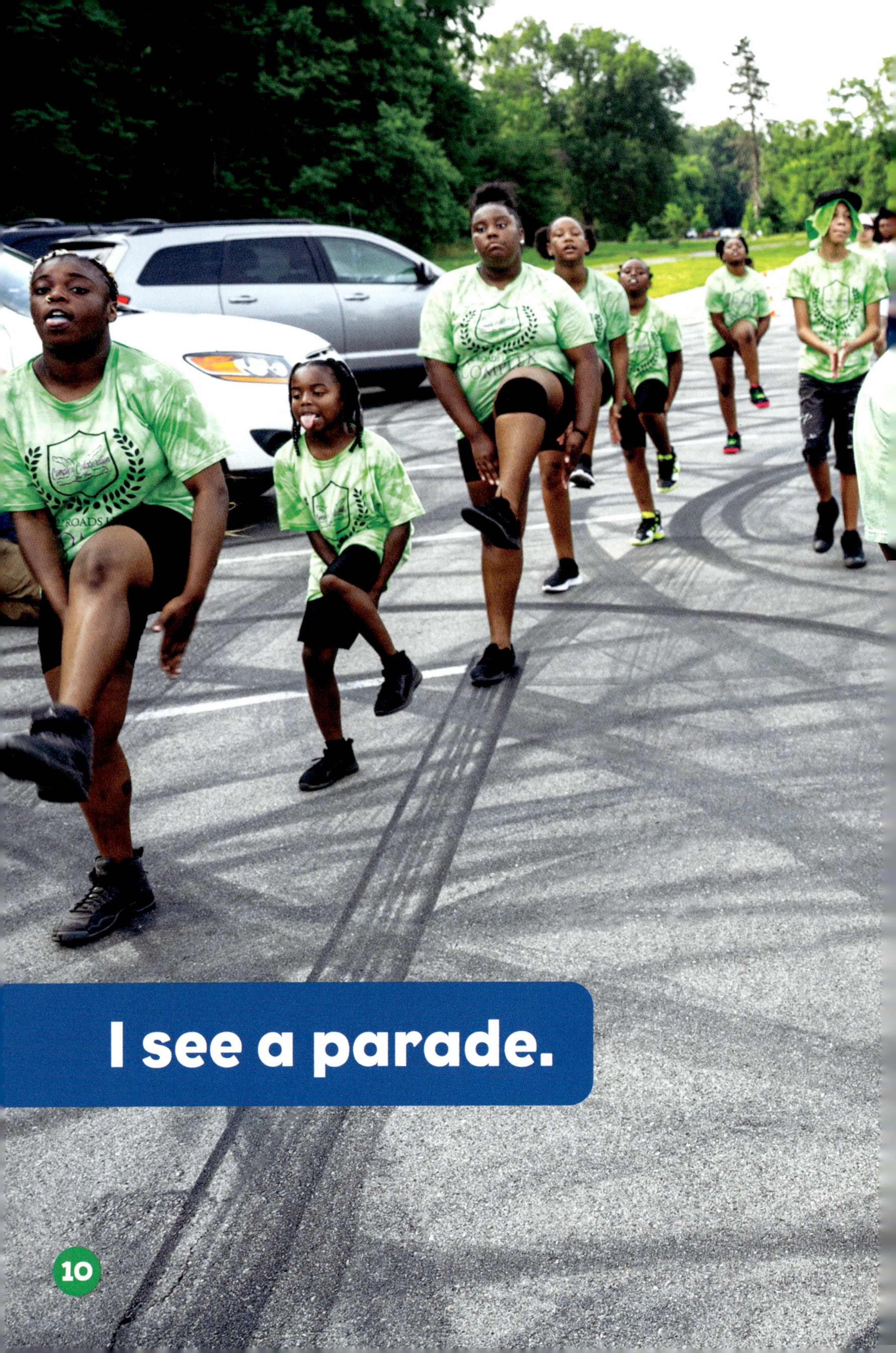

I see a parade.

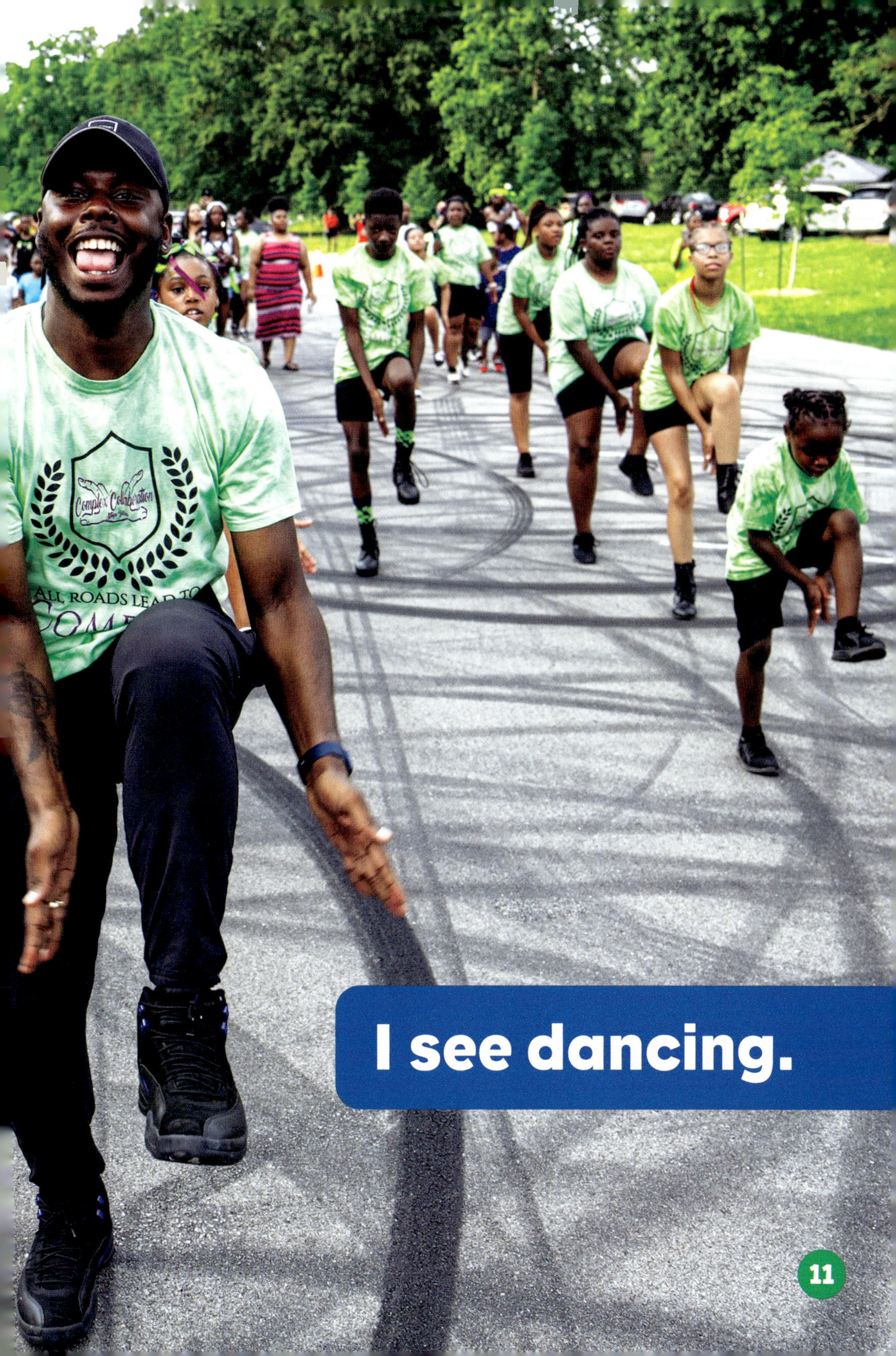

I see dancing.

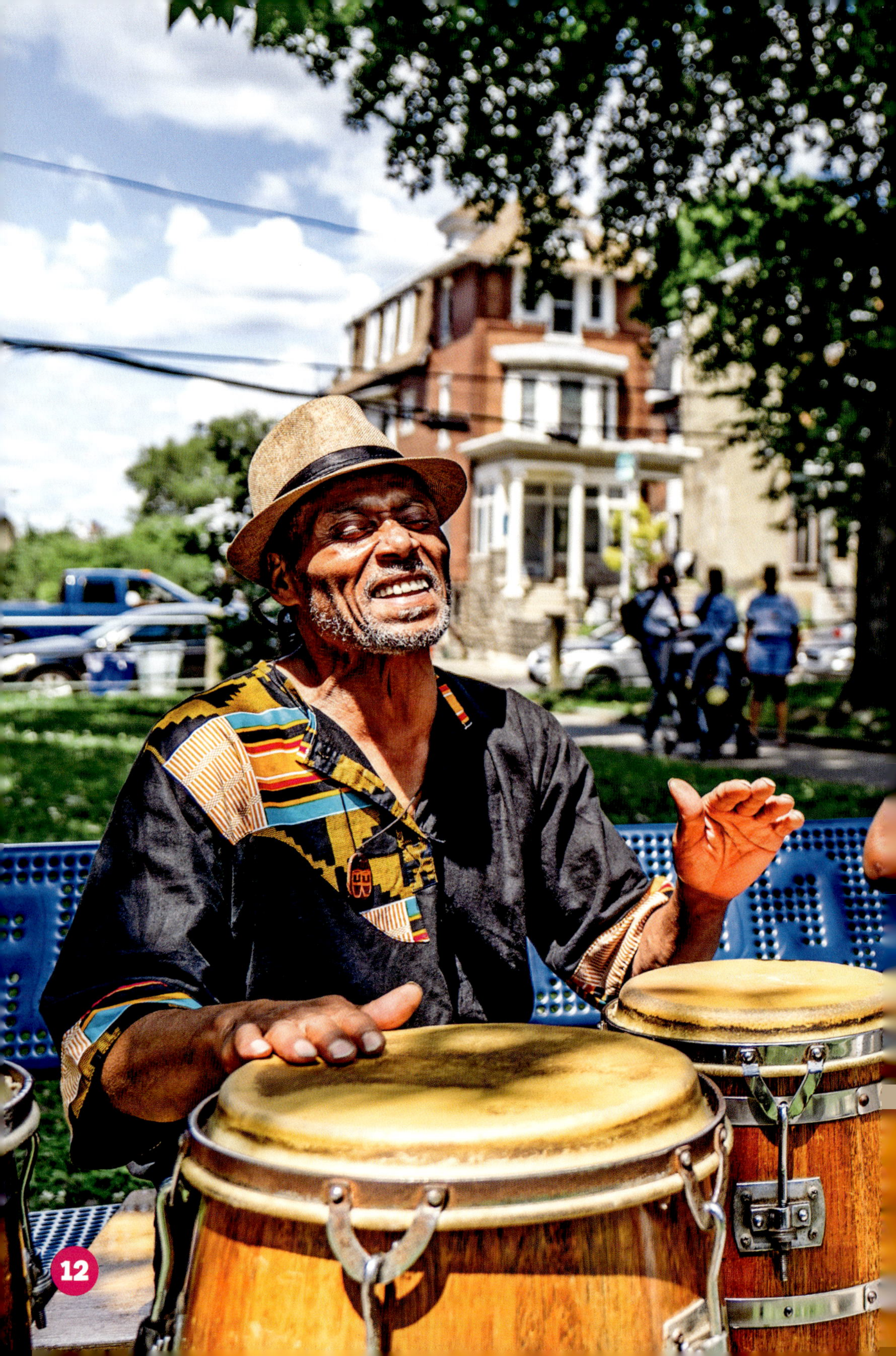

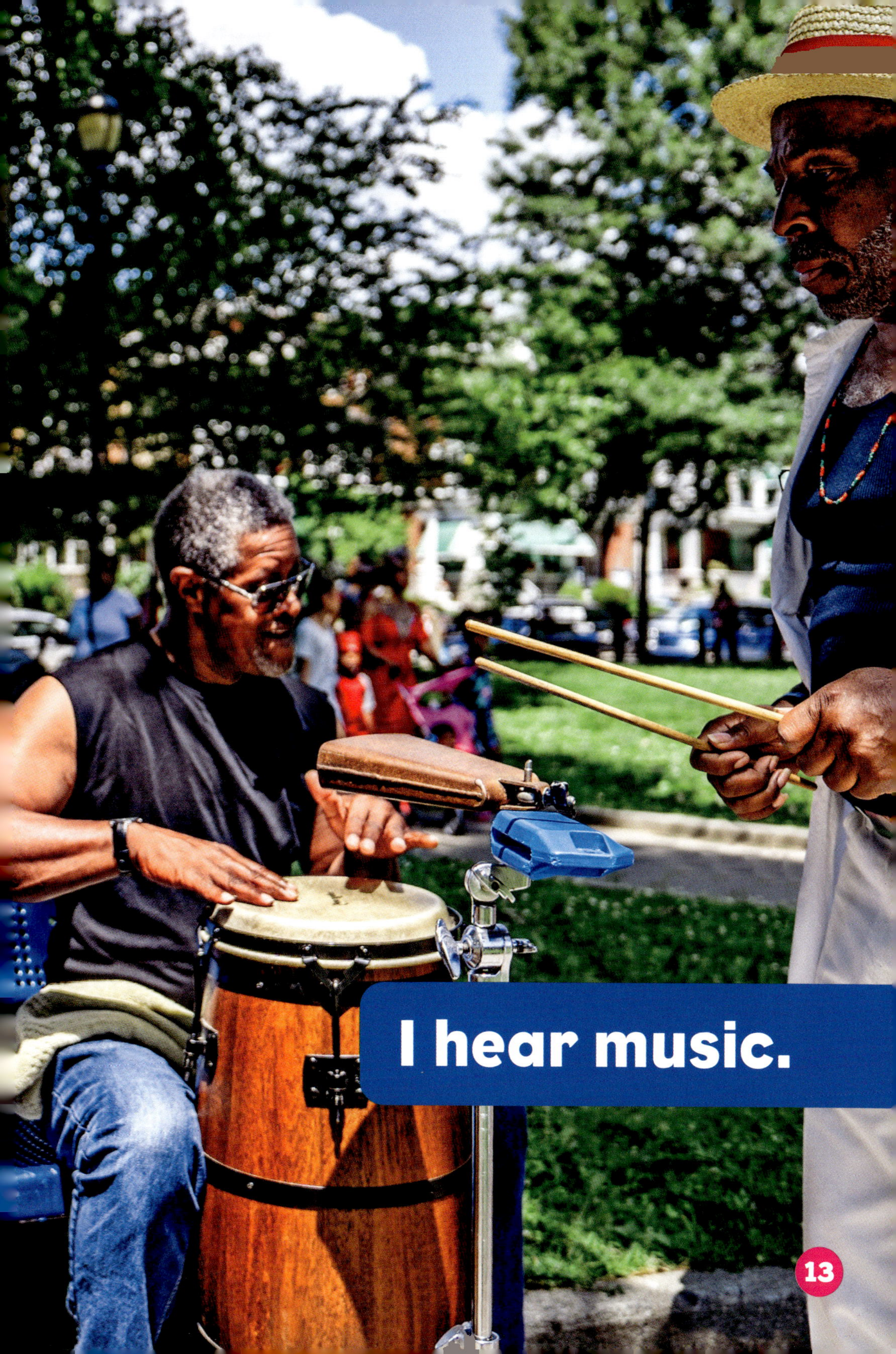

I hear music.

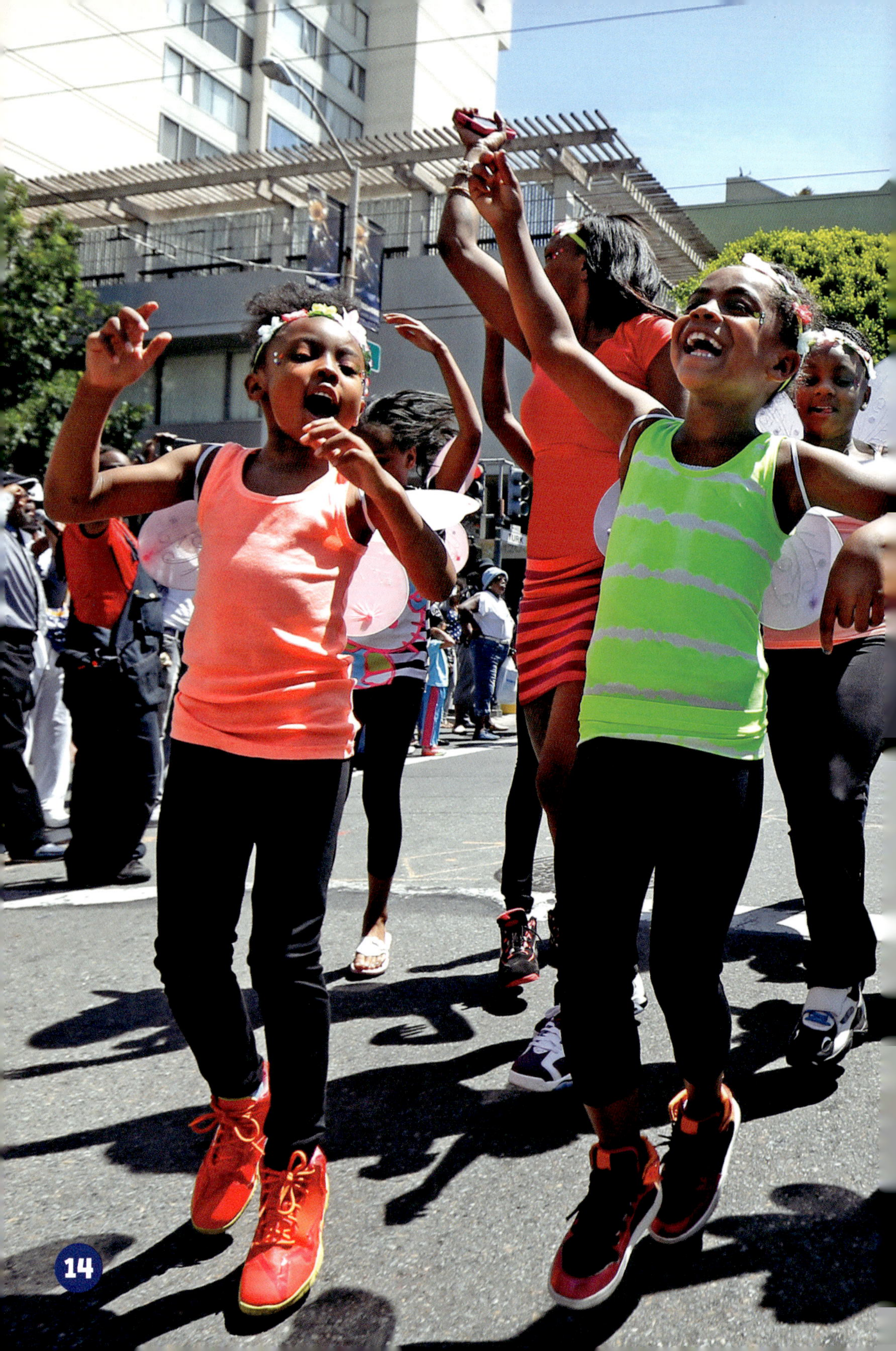

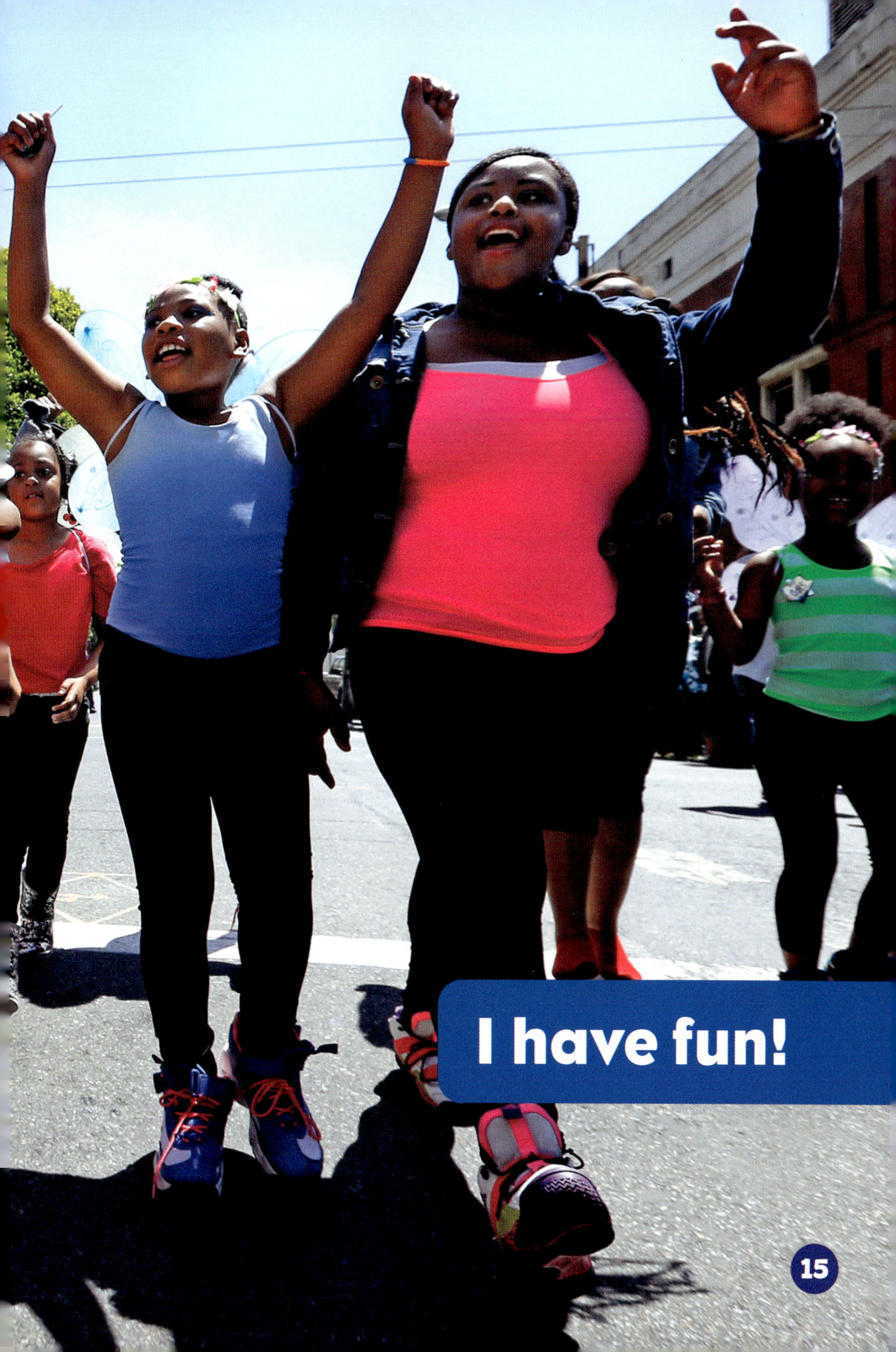

I have fun!

LET'S REVIEW!

Juneteenth is June 19. It celebrates Black Americans' freedom. How is this family celebrating?

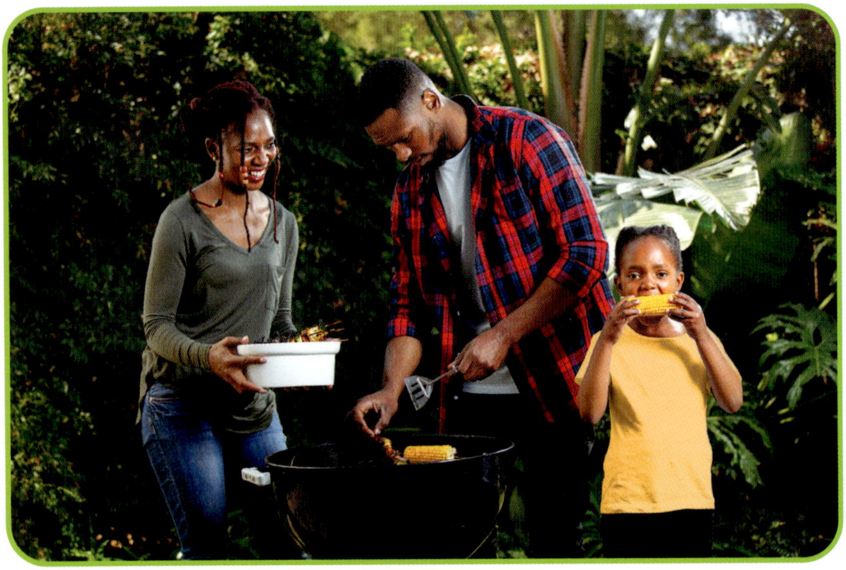

INDEX